pictures of health

Noreen Wetton   **Margaret Collins**

Acknowledgements

The authors and publishers would like to thank the children and staff at Sealand Primary School, Stanney Grange Primary School and Parkgate Primary School for their enthusiasm and commitment in generating display work to support this book. A special thank you is also given to the children and staff at Nicholas Hawksmoor Primary School, St Martin's (C of E) Infant School, Orchard Infant School and White's Wood Lane Community Junior School for their contributions towards the display work in *Pictures of Health*.

The publishers would particularly like to thank Rob Golding, Michelle Fox, Meic Griffiths and Marjorie Downey for their help in the organisation of the artwork.

Finally, the authors would like to thank the Research and Graduate School of Education at the University of Southampton for its continued support in their projects.

The Colour of Feelings (page 14)

First published in 2003 by BELAIR PUBLICATIONS LIMITED

Apex Business Centre, Boscombe Road, Dunstable, Beds, LU5 4RL

© 2003 Folens on behalf of the authors Noreen Wetton and Margaret Collins

Commissioning Editor: Zoë Nichols

Editor: Nancy Candlin

Layout artist: Suzanne Ward

Design: Lee Williams

Cover design: Duncan McTeer

Illustrator: Margaret Welbank, p55 and p64

Photography: Roger Brown, Marcus Pomfret and Kelvin Freeman

Being Friends (in Choices) by Althea. Published by A&C Black. Reproduced by permission of A&C Black; Who Are Your Friends? (in All About You) by Jillian Powell. Published by Hodder Wayland. Reproduced by permission of Hodder and Stoughton Limited; Being Kind (in Growing Up) by Janine Amos and Annabel Spenceley. Published by Cherry Tree Books; Taking Turns (in Growing Up) by Janine Amos and Annabel Spenceley. Published by Cherry Tree Books; Where's My Teddy? (in Managing Change) by Jez Alborough. Published by Walker Books. Reproduced by permission of the publisher Walker Books Ltd, London; Badger's Parting Gifts (in Managing Change) by Susan Varley. Published by Collins Picture Lions

Printed in 2003

Reprinted 2004

ISBN 0-94788-295-2

Contents

Introduction

Welcome to *Pictures of Health*. This book provides a starting point for the teaching of PSHE/Citizenship. It contains practical activities that can be adapted across the age range 5–11. We hope the book will help you to motivate children and lead to quality work in PSHE/Citizenship that culminates in interactive, eye-catching displays.

Current research sees the development of life skills as the key to healthy lifestyles. The responsibility of schools is to develop these life skills, starting as soon as children begin their education. Health in this context includes aspects of physical, mental and emotional well being, a sense of self-worth, positive relationships and the motivation to learn. These skills are addressed through the themes of each chapter, emphasising the key role of language in enabling children to practise and consolidate their learning.

The life skills emphasised in this book include:

- a growing awareness of the needs of their own bodies
- a growing awareness of the impact of their own behaviour on others
- an ability to empathise with others and see the world from a different point of view
- a growing understanding of relationships and friendships
- a growing language to describe their changing lifestyles and their health
- a growing sense of self-worth and self-esteem as emerging citizens
- a growing awareness of their place in the world and responsibilities in keeping our environment clean and safe.

The themes are developed and reinforced through a variety of activities. Children are encouraged to talk and write about their opinions and then present their findings in a creative way. We demonstrate how teachers can use the children's work to produce stimulating displays appropriate to their age and stage of development.

Several themes are linked to examples of children's literature, and some activities begin with a story that is used to reinforce the key concepts. Full details of the titles used in this book and other recommended stories are listed on page 70. It is likely that you will want to add to this list.

Display – a resource

Once you have created a display, it is important to make full use of it. Use the display interactively. Encourage children to return to the display to reread and add to it. Motivate the class to use the display as a resource. Reflect on it, reminding the children to put their learning into action.

Finally, share your display! Use the ideas as the basis for an assembly. Invite visitors from other classes, home and the wider community to come to celebrate the learning that underpins the displays.

Noreen Wetton and *Margaret Collins*

Friends are all around us

Focus of Learning

Increasing awareness of the role of friendship in people's lives

Starting Points

- Ask the children to think about the friends they have in and out of school. (Be sensitive to children who may have no friends.)
- Invite the class to bring in photographs of themselves and some of their friends, and contribute your own photographs.

Activities

- Sort the photographs into groups, with headings such as 'Animals', 'Children' and 'Adults'.

MY FRIEND MEGHAN
Meghan is my very best friend because we always play together.
The little boys sometimes chase us but we are still best friends. Sometimes we play together but some times we don't. When we do fall out it's not for very long. If we are not busy after school we go to each others houses.
We sit next to each other in school if we can.
Sometimes we make very good secrets between us.
I like Meghan.

- Suggest the children paint or make pastel pictures of their friends, and then write about what a friend means to them and what they do together.

- Look again at the photographs and ask the class to say what makes a person a friend, writing down their ideas. Share the writing in a class poem about all kinds of friends using the children's ideas. You could start the poem 'A friend is …'.

MY FRIEND ALFIE
I like Alfie because he is funny and he is kind. Alfie always plays games with me. We play fun games like bulldog.
He saves me a space next to him in class when he can. Alfie is always happy and he doesn't often get cross. We laugh a lot together. I know Alfie would cheer me up if ever I got sad.
Kwan Walley

- Write a 'Recipe for friendship' including the children's ideas about what makes a good friend.
- Read stories about friendships, such as *Just Like Us* by Hiawyn Oram (published by Corgi). Encourage the children to look for other stories about friends and friendships (see page 70).
- Display the children's writing about friends surrounded by the paintings.
- Make a table display of 'friend' stories. Help the class to write book reviews or design posters to add to the display.

The friend shop

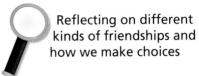

Focus of Learning

Reflecting on different kinds of friendships and how we make choices

Starting Points

- Remind the class of the different friends they have, including people older and younger than themselves, neighbours and pets.
- Talk about how some people make friends more quickly than others, and how some prefer to have lots of friends while others choose just one.

Activities

- Prompt the children to tell you what they think makes a good friend. Write their ideas on individual cards.
- Sit in a circle and place the cards in the middle. Ask the children to imagine that the centre of the circle is a 'friend shop' and that the cards represent the friends for sale. Explain that at the friend shop they can buy a wide variety of friends with many different personalities.
- Look at the cards and ask the class to think about the kind of friend they would prefer. Which friend would they choose? Why would they choose this friend? Would they buy several friends or just one?
- Ask for two or three volunteers to go into the shop to 'buy' a friend. Encourage them to explain the reasons behind their choices. Stress the importance of respecting and listening to the views of others.
- Make a model of the friend shop. Cut out figures from cardboard and dress them using dolls' clothes and collage materials. Give the figures names, for example 'Share', 'Care' and 'Friendly'.
- Make the shop front from decorated cardboard and display the figures inside and outside the shop, with notices about what kinds of friends are on offer.

What is a friend?

Focus of Learning

Explaining the importance of friendship

Starting Points

- Tell the story of an alien who has fallen to earth and doesn't know anything about friends and friendship.
- Ask the children how they would explain to the alien what a good friend is, what good friends do and don't do, and what they say and don't say. Make a list of their views.

Activities

- With the class, make the alien from junk boxes and paint on its features.
- Ask the children to paint some large pictures to show the alien all the things from the 'Starting points' list that good friends do, are and say, to explain that friendship is important to our people.
- Display the children's paintings around the alien with labels explaining what it means to be a good friend.

- Talk with the class about the kinds of friends they themselves would choose. Explain that we all have different personalities; some of us make friends more quickly than others, some prefer to have lots of friends, and some enjoy having just one special friend.

Postcards from Earth

- Talk with the children about the things they enjoy doing with their friends – indoors and outdoors, in summer and winter, at home and at school. Collect these ideas under different headings.

- Read *Dr Xargles Book of Earthlets* by Jeanne Willis (published by Red Fox), in which a class of alien schoolchildren, in disguise, visit planet Earth. Their interpretations are logical and amusing, and are a good starting point for looking at and respecting differences and misinterpretations of other people's lifestyles.

Focus of Learning

Clarifying friendship to other people

Activities

- As a class, create an imaginary planet on which aliens live. Imagine that these aliens know nothing about friendship and that the children need to explain to them the qualities of a good friend. Ask the children what life must be like for the aliens without friends.

- Make a 3-D alien planet from different types of paper. Paint the planet and the aliens that live on it. Add keywords around the planet indicating the qualities of a friend. Use the children's ideas listed earlier.

- Ask the children to write postcards to the aliens to tell them what a good friend is and does. Display these postcards on the planet.

Networks

- Introduce the idea of working together in your class as being like a network in which each person is linked to everybody else by invisible threads.

- Illustrate this by giving one group a length of coloured wool to hold, to link each child. Ask the children to demonstrate what happens to the group when someone leaves. It affects the others in the group.

- Discuss what happens in the network when someone is angry, upset, unkind, selfish, will not co-operate or will not do his or her share. How does it make others in the network feel? 'What could you do if your network was in trouble?'

Focus of learning

Recognising that our actions affect ourselves and others

Activities

- Challenge the children to make a set of network rules to encourage empathetic behaviour and to help them work together. For example, 'Take turns', 'Say please', 'Think of others' and 'Help each other'.

- Encourage the class to think about their own personal networks, and to draw themselves at the centre and their network of people around them.

- Collect network words (such as 'Relatives', 'Crowd', 'Team', 'Choir', 'Club' and 'Class') to display around the children's pictures.

- In groups, suggest the children paint large pictures to illustrate these network groups. Display the paintings joined together with coloured thread or lines and the network rules.

10

Lost and lonely

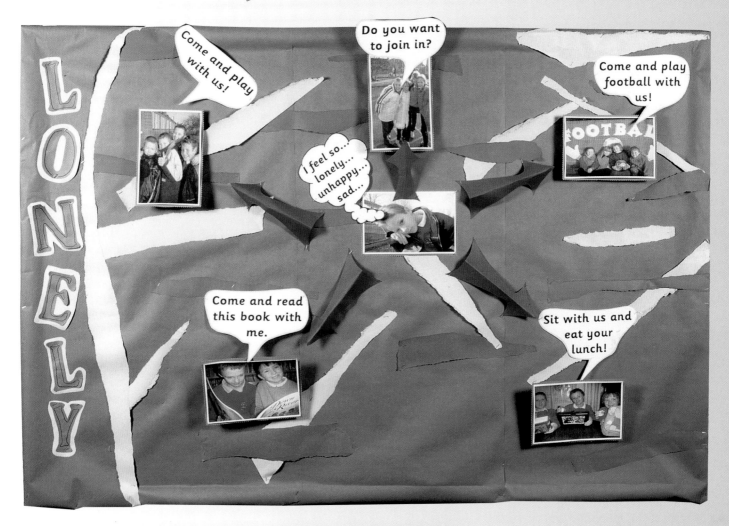

Focus of Learning

Recognising other people's feelings and seeing things from another point of view

Come and read this book with me.

Starting Points

- Ask the children to listen to the following scenario: 'A new child at your school is always alone in the playground, never talking to or playing with other children.' How does the class think this new child feels?
- Invite the children to help you to make a list of 'feelings' words.

Activities

- Ask each group to take photographs or to paint pictures of their group enjoying different activities in the playground. Display these with a picture of the new child in the centre.
- Help the children to write speech bubbles to show what they would say and do, and how they would persuade others to include the lonely child in their play. Add a thought bubble to the lonely child, describing how he or she is feeling.
- This activity could be extended through drama and could be used with the children in formulating a playground policy.

All kinds of families

Focus of Learning

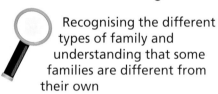

Recognising the different types of family and understanding that some families are different from their own

Starting Points

- Ask the children to start a collection of pictures and photographs showing all kinds of families, including their own.
- Explain that a family can be of any size, for example, big, very big, small, very small, far away, people who live alone.
- It is important to remind the children that families are all different.

Activities

- Invite the children to paint pictures of their families. Display the pictures on a wall labelled 'Our family album'.
- Use the display to talk about family relationships and what helps to keep family life happy.
- Talk about the things that cause families to worry and argue. Collect the words the children use in 'emotion' books and talk about what the family can do to put things right.
- Make masks showing the emotions and display them with the books.

A family tree

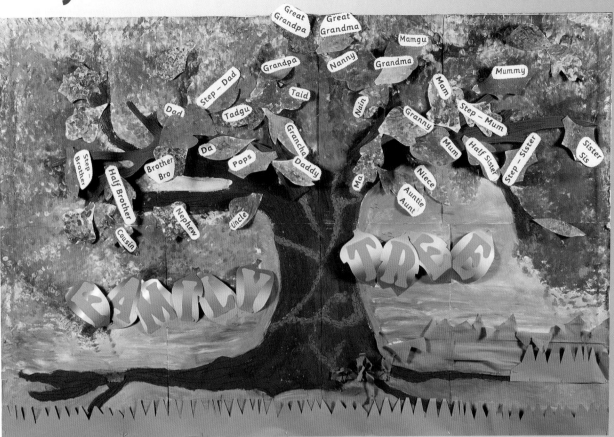

Starting Points

- Talk with the children about all the different people in families. Who are they? What do we call them? (For example, 'Granny', 'Nanny', 'Grandma', 'Gran', 'Grandma Jenny', 'Grandma Smith'.)
- Make a list of these words on the whiteboard.

Focus of Learning

 Recognising that people of all ages make a family

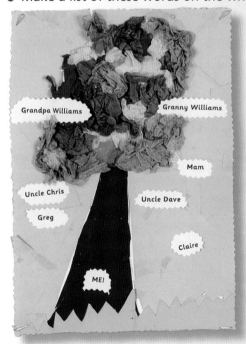

Activities

- With the children's help, write all the names onto cards.
- As a group, sort the words into sets (for example, put all the grandad words together).
- Work as a class to arrange the sets in order, from the most senior to youngest.
- Paint and make a collage of a very large tree. Put the names onto the tree in descending order of seniority, with the oldest person at the top.
- Can the class add any more words at the top? Can they add any more words at the bottom?
- Ask the children to make a collage of individual trees and to add labels that are specific to their family (for example, 'Grandma White', 'Aunty Margaret'), in order of seniority. While the children are doing this, go round and talk about how each family is different. Celebrate all families, large or small.

The colour of feelings

- Ask the children to show with their faces and bodies how they look when they are surprised, excited, sad, lonely, afraid and angry.

Focus of Learning

Expressing feelings through colour

- Look at the work of some artists who use colour to express feelings, such as Vincent Van Gogh's and Mark Rothko.

- Talk about colours to do with feelings for example; red for anger, blue for sadness, etc. Ask the children to paint pictures with colours that show these feelings.

- As a class, look at the contrasting paintings and try and guess the mood conveyed in each one.

- Display the paintings with labels explaining the children's thoughts and feelings. Add lift-the-flap labels to reveal each feeling.

A volcano of feelings

Starting Points

- Ask the children what makes them cross. Prompt them to make a face to show how they look when something has made them cross.
- Now ask the class to make a face to show how they look when they are really angry. How is this different from when they were cross?

Focus of Learning

Recognising and dealing with feelings of anger

Activities

- Encourage the children to draw faces to illustrate feeling cross and angry. Using different coloured pens, add words to describe their feelings in speech bubbles.
- Ask the children to think about a time when they felt angry. Where in their bodies did they feel the angry feelings? How does it feel to be angry? (For example, hot, jumpy, wanting to shout, cry and run.)
- Make a collage of a volcano with words to go with angry feelings bursting from the top.
- Ask the children to think of ways of managing their angry feelings and calming down. Remind them that they are in charge of their feelings.

How do I show feelings?

- Ask the children what they think it means when someone says, 'I feel blue today'. Can they show with their faces and bodies how someone feeling 'blue' would look?

- Talk about other expressions such as 'red-faced', 'green with envy', 'purple with rage'. What do these phrases really mean? Have the children ever felt like this? What did it make them want to do? Who or what made them feel better?

Activities

- Illustrate some of these colour expressions by painting faces to depict the different types of feelings. Use collage for the hair and facial features.

- Make a background for the display on separate large sheets of paper. Using different colours of paint for each sheet, encourage the class to show different feelings through a variety of techniques. For example, red splatters for anger, green handprints for envy, gentle yellow waves for happy.

- Stick the painted faces onto the appropriate background. Ask the children to add speech bubbles next to each face explaining how they are feeling and why.

Focus of Learning

Exploring ways of illustrating and sharing feelings

16

Capture the mood

Sunshine Happy

- Look at portraits painted by Pablo Picasso and Vincent Van Gogh, where the artists have tried to show people's feelings through colour.
- How have the artists used other ways as well as colour to show people's feelings? Do the eyes, mouth or hands contribute to the effect?

Happiness is bright yellow like the sun.

It smells like sweets from a famous shop.

Happiness tastes like a baked cake straight from the oven.

It sounds like a late party in the night.

It feels like a bouncy castle at a fair.

Happiness lives in the sun.

Activities

- Ask the class to use the artists' work as a basis for their own paintings of portraits.
- Try to encourage children to exaggerate the mood portrayed by using only the shades of one colour, for example yellow for happiness, blue for sadness, green for jealousy.
- Add collage materials in the same colour.
- Invite the children to compose poems using similes to suit the mood of the portraits.

Focus of Learning

Exploring feelings and mood expressed in colour

Don't be afraid

Exploring ways of dealing with fears

Starting Points

- Talk to the children about things that people fear. Some of these fears may be real, such as a fear of the dark, or imaginary, such as a fear of monsters.
- Collect their ideas and group them into two sections: 'Real fears' and 'Fantasy fears'.

Activities

- Discuss what the children do when they are afraid. Do they shout out, go to someone else's room, hide, put the light on?
- Ask the children to paint a picture on a large sheet of paper illustrating their fears.

- Display the paintings and discuss as a group how you could help someone overcome their fears. Ideas might include 'talking to an adult' or 'turning on a light'. Write the children's suggestions next to the paintings.
- Follow up this work later by asking the children if any of the suggestions have helped them deal with their fears.

The owl who was afraid of the dark

Focus of learning

Recognising that everyone is afraid sometimes and learning ways of dealing with fears

Starting Points

- Read *The Owl Who Was Afraid of the Dark* by Jill Tomlinson (published by Mammoth Books).

- Ask the children what made Plop afraid of the dark and collect some vocabulary to describe his feelings, for example 'scared', 'small', 'frightened' and 'terrified'.

- Talk about why the other characters featured in the story were not afraid of the dark.

- Prompt the children for suggestions to help Plop face his fears.

Activities

- Discuss Plop's feelings at the end of the story. Is he still scared? What has made him feel better?

- Make a 3D display to illustrate the story. Use junk and collage materials to make the three owls. Make a 3D tree and paint a night-time backdrop.

- Display words that describe Plop's feelings in stars around the display. Add speech bubbles near the owls containing the children's advice to Plop.

- Ask the children to work in pairs to write down who and what helped them to overcome a fear that they had when they were younger.

When is it bullying?

Focus of Learning

Understanding the difference between bullying and everyday disagreements

- Talk to the class about what is meant by teasing, joking and bullying, and how they are all different.
- Discuss situations that occur which are not bullying, for example, one-off arguments or accidentally hurting somebody.
- Make it clear to the children that bullying is deliberately hurtful behaviour, which is repeated over a period of time.

Activities

- Help the children to devise a simple role-play to show the difference between everyday disagreements and bullying.
- Talk about how bullies can be anybody, not just confident people. Discuss why the person becomes a bully, including the reasons behind the bullying, such as gaining power.
- Discuss the school's policy on bullying so that the children know what to do if they are bullied or if they see bullying occur in school.

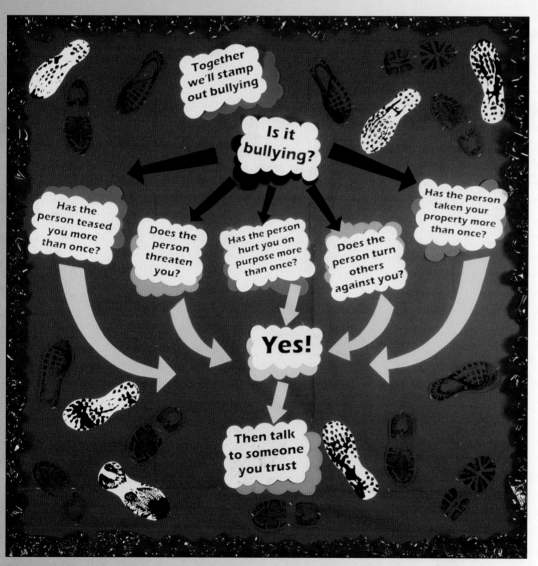

- Create a display of colourful bubbles and arrows. Inside the bubbles, write the questions the children can ask to help them decide whether what has happened is bullying. In one big bubble, emphasise the importance of telling a trusted person as a way of dealing with bullying.

Let's make our school a bully-free zone

Focus of Learning

Recognising the effects of bullying and understanding what action to take against it

Starting Points

- Invite the children to draw a picture of someone who has been bullied and to say how that person feels. Collect their vocabulary, such as 'Why me?', 'Is it my own fault?', 'Lonely', 'Hurt feelings'.

Activities

- Role-play a situation in which the children witness somebody being bullied. What could they do to help the bullied child? How could they make the bullies see that what they were doing was not teasing but bullying? Make a list of the children's advice, such as 'Talk to an adult', 'Say, "Leave her alone"', 'Don't join in with bullying' and 'Stick with us'.
- Ask the class how they would persuade other people to help them stop the bullying.
- Suggest the children use paper plates and other materials to make collages of faces. Display these with speech bubbles telling everyone how the class makes sure that their school is a bully-free zone.

Circle of life

Focus of Learning

Understanding how we change as we grow up

Starting Points

- Read *Once There Were Giants* by Martin Waddell (published by Walker Books) and ask the children to think about how the character changes throughout the story.

- Discuss how, in the story, the girl's body changes over time and how the changes seem to happen without anyone noticing.

- Talk with the children about the first and last pictures. How are they the same and how are they different?

- Chat briefly about where the children fit into the story. Can they remember feeling like the character when they were younger?

Activities

- Use the first picture to introduce the concept of a life cycle or 'The circle of life'.

- Can the children remember being smaller – in a world full of giants? How did it feel? Do they still think adults are giants?

- Ask the children to draw themselves in a circle of life, labelling each stage.

- Make a display to show the different stages of life. Sew faces and make collages of bodies for each stage. Add arrow labels to show how we grow from being a baby to adulthood.

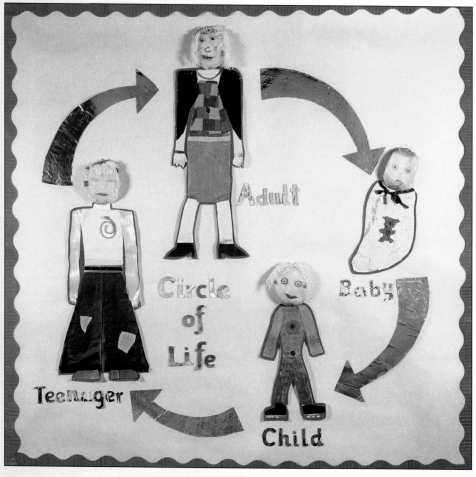

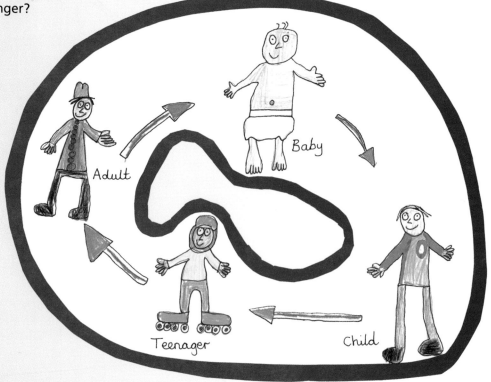

Caring for a baby

Focus of Learning

Widening understanding of the long-term responsibilities of caring for a baby

Starting Points

- Talk about the excitement of knowing there is a new baby growing inside its mother. How do we know what is happening inside? Explain that ultrasound scans are used to see how the baby is developing, and to see when it might be born.

Activities

- Talk to the class about the things babies need, such as homes, love and families. Discuss the hard work involved in looking after a baby. What do parents have to do? Ask the children to illustrate the needs of a baby in pictures and in writing.

- Read older children extracts from *Flour Babies* by Anne Fine (published by Puffin Books). The flour babies are bags of flour, which children have to care for night and day over a given time. Gradually, the flour baby carers become aware of some of the long-term responsibilities of parenthood.

- Discuss how the class would feel if they had to care for a baby day and night.

- Add the children's pictures and writing to the display alongside any other pictures and information that they may have found about babies.

Growing up

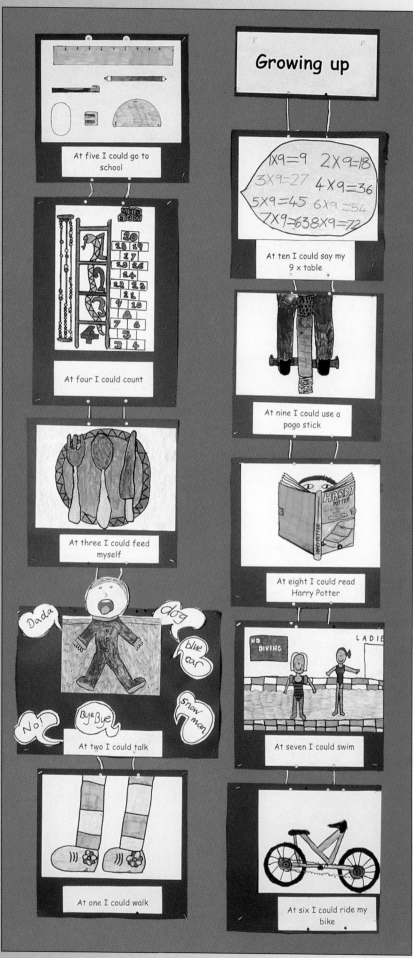

At five I could go to school

At four I could count

At three I could feed myself

Dada / dog / blue car / Snow man / No! / Bye Bye

At two I could talk

At one I could walk

Growing up

$$1 \times 9 = 9 \quad 2 \times 9 = 18$$
$$3 \times 9 = 27 \quad 4 \times 9 = 36$$
$$5 \times 9 = 45 \quad 6 \times 9 = 54$$
$$7 \times 9 = 63 \quad 8 \times 9 = 72$$

At ten I could say my 9 x table

At nine I could use a pogo stick

At eight I could read Harry Potter

At seven I could swim

At six I could ride my bike

Focus of Learning

Increasing understanding of new skills as they grow up

Starting Points

- Read the poem 'The End' by A A Milne. Talk with the children about what they were able to do at different ages. Discuss how we grow and change every year. What can they do now that they couldn't do a few years ago?

Activities

- Ask each child to illustrate themselves at different ages on separate squares of paper. Encourage them to think carefully about something different they could do at each age of their life. For example, when they were one they started to walk, when they were two they could talk, and so on.
- Join the squares together to make a wall hanging for each child.
- To each square, add the age and a label describing what the child was able to do.
- Invite the class to bring in photographs showing themselves at different ages. Talk about how their appearance has changed. Display these photographs alongside the wall hangings.

Memories

Starting Points

- Talk about things that the children remember from when they were younger. Invite a volunteer to sit on a 'memory chair' and recall a past experience to share with the rest of the group. Encourage the other class members to listen well and to ask questions.

My memory is of a garden in Spain when I was on my holiday. There were lots of different flowers and lots of pretty colours on the flowers in the Spanish garden.

Activities

- Talk about how we remember both happy and sad events in the past. List the children's past memories under headings that reflect their feelings about these memories, for example, 'Funny things', 'Happy things' and 'Scary things'.

- Discuss how the children keep their memories – perhaps as stories, videos, photographs or diaries. You might read *Wilfred Gordon McDonald Partridge* (published by Puffin Books), about a character who collects memories for someone who has lost theirs.

- Ask the children to think of a memory that makes them feel happy. Help them to make a 'memory cushion' using two squares of material. On one square, make a collage or sew a picture that will remind the child of that memory. For example, a bucket and spade could be cut out from felt to remind a child of a happy memory at the beach.

- Sew the two squares together leaving a small gap along one side. Fill with stuffing. Sew up the gap.

- Display the cushions together with the children's memories about past experiences.

Focus of Learning

 Understanding the importance of memory to themselves and other people

How we know we are growing

Focus of Learning

Looking for evidence that our bodies are growing and changing

Activities

- Ask if the children have had new shoes recently and record their responses. Think about who has gone up a shoe size and what sizes they are now.
- Work in groups to conduct a survey relating to one of the above points. Collect data from children in the class and discuss ways of presenting their findings to inform other people. You might use ICT to generate a graph.
- Make a display that demonstrates growth. Draw around and cut out an infant's, a junior's and a teacher's shoe. Display these together with a jumper, trousers and handprints to match each size.

Starting Point

- Talk about how the children can tell that they are growing. For example, outgrowing clothes or shoes, being able to reach things they couldn't before, and so on.

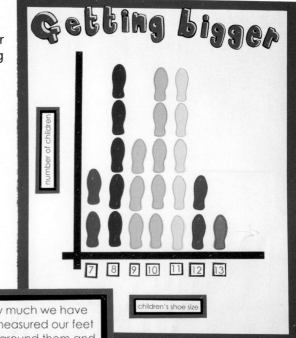

To see how much we have grown we measured our feet by drawing around them and recorded our findings on this graph.

Body image

Focus of Learning

Understanding that there is no 'right' way to look and that it is important to feel happy about oneself

Challenging media images

Starting Points

- Talk with the children about whether their bodies grow suddenly or gradually, how we all have our own growth patterns and how different people grow at different times.

- Discuss how we would all like to change something about the way we look. Talk about the 'perfect' images portrayed in the media. How does the media show young girls or boys? Ask the children to challenge these views. (Use this as an opportunity to talk about the dangers of dieting.)

Activities

- Celebrate 'being you'. Talk with the children about how they can walk tall, look good and feel good about themselves, rather than change themselves to look like people in the media.

  - In a group, give everyone the opportunity to say one thing that they like about themselves.

  - Illustrate these points in a class jigsaw display. Ask the children to make a self-portrait collage and to add speech bubbles showing what they like about themselves. Place the jigsaw pieces together to create a complete class record of positive statements about each child.

Feeling good

The image shows the following labels on the flower petals and leaves:
- Be helpful
- Be friend[ly]
- Be generous
- Take turns
- Share things
- Care for each other
- Say "Good morning"
- Smile at each other
- Listen to each other
- We are trying to follow the leaves and make our school a happy place to be

Starting Points

- Prompt the children to think about all the things that make them feel good in school and in the classroom, especially the things people do and say. Collect these ideas.

- How can we make people feel good in our class or school? Talk about how the children's own behaviour can help to make a happy environment.

Focus of Learning

Emphasising that how we behave contributes to a happy environment

Activities

- Ask the children to make an illustrated list of all their ideas for making the school a happier place. Does it include being friendly, helpful, listening to others, sharing?

- Make a large sunflower head from card and yellow and brown tissue paper. Make a large stalk from rolled up green crêpe paper. Add large green paper leaves and staple these up the stalk.

- Make a 3D plant pot from card painted brown.

- Ask the children to write labels, one for each leaf, showing their ideas for making their school a happier place.

Feeling better

Starting Points

- Give the children an opportunity to share experiences of when they have felt hurt or unhappy.
- Talk about how other people sometimes hurt or upset our feelings.
- Discuss ways of dealing with situations that make the children feel unhappy. Who would they go to for help? What would they say to this person? Write their suggestions on the whiteboard.

Activities

- Chat about other ways of making yourself feel better, such as playing with friends, listening to music and exercising.
- On two circles of card, make a collage or paint a picture of a happy and a sad face. Fold a sheet of paper in half. Stick the sad face on the front with the words 'When I feel sad … '. Under the flap stick the happy face and ask the children to write one way that they could make themselves feel better.

Looking to the future

Starting Points

- Ask the children to think about being grown up and the job they would like to do.
- Invite them to draw a quick picture of themselves doing this job.

Focus of Learning

Comparing dreams, reality and the skills needed for future work

Activities

- Share the children's views and pictures and challenge any gender stereotyping.
- What would they have to learn to be able to do this job? Make a list of some of these skills, for example, sing, dance, play an instrument, fly a plane.
- Suggest the class uses books and the Internet to find out more about these jobs.
- Make a display to show the 'dream' jobs. Ask the children to draw large figures and paint on the skin and features before making a collage of the hair, clothes and any accessories that are associated with the job.
- Display the figures with labels showing the different types of job.
- Invite visitors in to talk about their jobs and make a list of questions to ask them.

Money, money, money

Focus of Learning

Heightening awareness of the role of money in people's lives and the importance of learning to manage money

Starting Points

- Ask the children to tell you why they think we have money. How would we manage if we didn't have money?
- Where do they think the money comes from to run the school? Who decides what to spend school money on and what to save up for?

Activities

- Discuss with the children who gives them money and what they do with it. Do they save any of it? Do they spend it all at once or do they make it last? What are they saving up for?

I am saving for a doll's house

I am saving for a hamster.

- Make an illustrated list of all the different places where people put their money when they want to save it, such as moneyboxes, safes, banks and building societies.
- Look at adverts on TV aimed at children. What are they trying to persuade you to buy?
- What advice would the children give to someone about saving up? Collect their suggestions.
- Talk about how important it is to plan what you do with your money because there isn't an endless supply.
- Make moneyboxes from papier-mâché. Display these with labels showing what the children hope to save for, and include the children's own advice for saving.

Lost and found

Starting Points

- Talk about the things that both you and the children have recently lost, for example, a purse, a ring or keys.
- How does it feel to lose something? Discuss how you feel when you find something you have lost – or if you never find it.
- Ask the children to bring a special toy to school to show the class. Talk about how they would feel if they lost their special toy.

Activities

- Read *Where's My Teddy?* by Jez Alborough (published by Walker Books). Talk about the end of the story and how the child and the teddy both felt when they were reunited.
- Invite the class to write about their own teddy or toy getting lost. How would they feel? Brainstorm some words under the two headings 'Lost' and 'Found' to describe their feelings. For example, 'upset', 'worried', 'scared', 'relieved', 'happy' and 'pleased'.
- Create a collage of a forest background. Ask each child to draw a bear. Hide the bear pictures between the trees in the forest. On one tree attach the word 'Lost' and add any words from the brainstorming session. Do the same with 'Found'. Add the book *Where's My Teddy* to the display.

Focus of Learning

Exploring feelings associated with loss

Remember me

- Talk about how it feels when people we care about go away for a little while, for a long time or forever. This could be an opportunity for the children to talk about the separation from, or the death of, a pet, a grandparent, another relative or a friend.

Focus of Learning

Exploring feelings of separation, loss and memories

Note: There could be situations in the children's lives that might cause them some concerns. You will know your children and their sensitivities and can adapt the introduction accordingly.

Activities

- Read *Badger's Parting Gifts* by Susan Varley (published by Collins Picture Lions). Tell the children that this is the story of some animal friends in which the oldest of them, Badger, knows that his body is wearing out and that soon he will die.

- Ask the children to think about how Badger's friends would feel when they knew he was going to leave them. Make sure that the children know its okay to feel sad, angry or upset when people go away and that it helps to talk about it.

- Discuss how the animals comforted each other and how Mole cried when Badger died. What helped the animals to feel less sad?

- Collect, make and display all the parting gifts that Badger left his friends. Have the children ever received a parting gift from someone?

Make a choice

- Tell the children the story of Sam and Jo (who could be boys or girls), who have been good friends since they started school. They've always played together and helped each other. One day they have a quarrel and stop being friends.

- Talk about how the story could end. Ask the children for some happy endings, some not so happy, and some sad or lonely endings.

- Then collect some suggestions for sorting out the quarrel.

Focus of Learning

Exploring how quarrels happen and finding ways to put things right

Activities

- Make 'choice' books. On the first page, children write about the cause of a quarrel. They should give the reader a choice of endings – for a happy ending, turn to page 2; for a sad ending, turn to page 3, and so on. Remind the class to write a different ending on each page.

- Ask the children to read their stories to the class, involving the other class members in the choice of ending that is read out.

- Make a 'choice' mobile. Ask the children to think of a scenario where there may have been a quarrel. Illustrate the argument and write what happened onto card. Make three ending cards with illustrations. Stick a piece of wooden dowel along the bottom of the argument card. Hang the three choices from arrows along the dowel. Add the words 'Make a choice' along the dowel and suspend the mobile from the ceiling.

- Use the mobiles to help sort out arguments that may occur over the next few weeks.

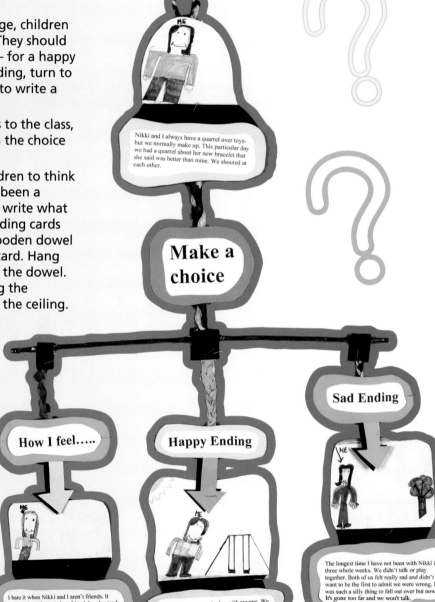

34

Breaking up and making up

Starting Points

- Ask the children about the times when they have fallen out with their friends. What were the reasons for the falling out? What did they say? How did they feel?

- Remind the class that just as it takes two people to quarrel, so it takes two people to make up.

- How did they make up again? Note their responses.

- Make a list of the different ways of making up, for example, talking about the problem, hugging and saying you are sorry. Which do they find is the best way to make up?

Focus of Learning

Discussing the causes of quarrels and explaining how to make up

Activities

- Divide a large display board in two. Paint a stormy sky onto one half and a light blue sky onto the other half. Explain that one half will represent how we feel when we are arguing, the other half when we are making up.

- Ask the children to make collages of thunderclouds and rain for the stormy half. Add labels to the clouds showing their feelings and responses to 'breaking up'.

- Add kites made from collage and a sun for the second half. Add the children's responses to 'making up' onto the kites.

- Remind the class to use the ideas on the kites to help resolve differences in the playground or out of school.

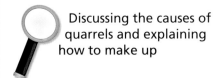

New families

- Introduce the children to four characters whose lives have changed: Mandy, Elvira, John and Tariq:
  - Mandy used to be an only child but she now has a new brother.
  - Grandma has come to live with Elvira's family.
  - John's mother has married again and he has a new family.
  - Tariq's big sister has come back home to live and everyone is making a big fuss of her.
- Discuss and list the good and not-so-good things about the changes in these four families.

Focus of Learning

Exploring ways of coping with changes in the family

Activities

- Look at the not-so-good things and ask the children to suggest ways to manage the changes so that everyone is happy. What advice would they give to the four people to make things happier? What advice would they give to other members of the different families?
- Display their advice around paintings of the four characters.
- Talk with the children about how sometimes changes happen in families and that it can take a while to get used to the new situations.

My goals

Starting Points

- Ask the children if there is anything they would like to change in the way they get on with people at home or in school.

- Explain to the class that changing things needs practice – like trying to get a netball in the net or a football in the goal.

- Point out that they need to practise before they can score a goal every time. Make a list of ways that might help to score a goal, such as 'If you fail, ask why and try again', 'Practise', 'Talk to people' and 'Listen to advice'.

Activities

- Talk about setting realistic targets for change and being able to accept failure.

- Prompt the children to write down something they would like to change in themselves on decorated cut-out ball shapes. Mount their target advice onto a real netball post or around a mini football goal.

Moving on

Focus of Learning

Looking back, looking forward and recognising personal achievements

Starting Points

- Ask the children to look back at themselves a year ago. What were they proud of, worried about and afraid of? How have they changed?
- Talk about the changes they think will take place in the next year. What might they worry about during that time? What are they looking forward to?

Activities

- Suggest the children write down all their old worries and 'post' them in a worry box set up in the classroom. Talk through the worries as a group and discuss ways of solving the problems. Remind the class that it is fine to feel anxious about starting something new. Stress the importance of talking to somebody they trust when they are worried.

- Invite the children to think of at least one achievement that they have been proud of in the last year. Praise their accomplishments, both big and small. Illustrate these achievements on circular paper and add crêpe paper borders to make a rosette. Display the rosettes, together with labels showing the children's successes.

38

All change

Focus of Learning

Encouraging a positive attitude to new challenges

Starting Points

- Ask the children to focus on the year ahead and the changes they expect. Are they changing classrooms or schools? What are they excited about? What are they anxious about? Who could help? Make a list of their ideas.

Activities

- Make boats from collage and junk materials. Add a mast with tissue-paper sails. On each sail, stick a 'change label' explaining something that the children are looking forward to in their new class or school.
- Make collage fish from different types of paper. On each fish suggest the children write a positive message of encouragement or advice to others who are worried about changing their class or school. Use the ideas listed earlier.
- Cover a display board with waves using blue paint and a variety of blue and transparent paper. Add the boats and fish to the display.

Keeping our bodies safe

Focus of Learning

Dealing positively with body contact

Starting Points

- Ask the children to think of times when they have been in a crowd with people pressing up against them, standing on their feet, elbowing them and pushing them. For example, in a shop, a queue or a market.
- Talk about how it felt and collect their vocabulary of feelings to describe this.
- Discuss whether getting angry or upset helps. Is it better to keep calm, to speak up, to shout or to ask people to be careful?

Activities

- Make a 'crowd' display of people queuing for an ice cream. Add life-size cardboard cut-out figures to the display to add a 3D effect.
- Prompt the class to suggest what the people bothered by the pushing might be saying. Add this to the display, either suspended on balloons or held up on placards.
- Remind the children that whether in a crowd or with just one person they have the right to say 'stop' to any kind of body contact which makes them feel uncomfortable, worried or frightened.

This is my body

Focus of Learning

Reminding children that they have the right to speak out about unacceptable body contact

Note: Be sensitive to any children who might reveal concerns about inappropriate touching.

Starting Points

- Gather the class into a tight group and discuss how it feels to be squashed in the middle of a crowd. How do they feel when they are being crowded or pushed? What do they want to say or shout out? Note their ideas.
- Talk to the children about body contact that makes them feel uncomfortable. Remind them that their bodies are theirs and they have the right to speak out if this happens.

Activities

- Read *Not Now Bernard* by David McKee (published by Red Fox). This is the story about Bernard who has not found the secret of making people stop, turn around and listen to him. What advice would the children give to Bernard?
- With the class, rehearse ways of getting an adult to stop, turn around and listen. Emphasise how important it is for children to go on telling the adult that they have been hurt until they have the adult's attention.
- Talk about the importance of finding a safe person they can trust and telling that person if someone's

hurting them in any way. (For example, pushing, pinching or any kind of touching that feels wrong or frightening.)
- Suggest the children draw an outline head and shoulders to represent themselves. Paint on skin tone and then add collage details to give 3D hair and facial features.
- Ask the class to think carefully about what they would say if they found themselves crowded or pushed, or in a situation that they felt was uncomfortable, worrying or frightening. How would they get someone to take notice of them? Collect their ideas and add these as a speech bubble statement next to their individual pictures.

Keeping safe out of school

Focus of Learning

Extending personal responsibility for keeping safe

Starting Points

- Talk with the class about the places they go to when they are not in school. Where do they go with their family? On their own? With their friends? Make a list of the places.

- As a class, decide on some simple safety rules to remember when out with friends, family or on their own.

Activities

- Create postcard-style images of the places where the children go.

- Invent symbols for safety rules in these places, draw the symbols and stick them onto the relevant places on the postcards.

- Talk about the positive things the children can do to help stay safe wherever they are. For example, knowing:
  - their names, addresses and telephone numbers
  - who is with them and being able to describe the person
  - who is in charge
  - an agreed place to meet if you get split up
  - how to get home, get help and shout for help
  - what the possible risks and dangers are.

- Role-play some scenarios and practise remembering personal information.

Emergency procedures

Starting Points

- Ask the children to tell you all the different places where they play, both in and out of school. Who do they go with? Who is in charge?

Activities

- Working in groups, invite each group to choose a different place and devise a set of rules for keeping safe when playing there.
- Display children's rules on warning triangles strung on a washing line across a corner of the classroom. Could any of the rules be applied to other places? Is there one piece of advice that would work for all the places where they play?
- Talk about what to do in an emergency. Do the children know what number to call?
- Ask groups of children to devise role-play scenarios showing what could happen in risky situations at some of the places they have chosen, and what to do in an emergency.
- Create a display with the emergency number as the focal point and large labels explaining what to do.

Focus of Learning

Understanding safety rules and learning what to do in an emergency

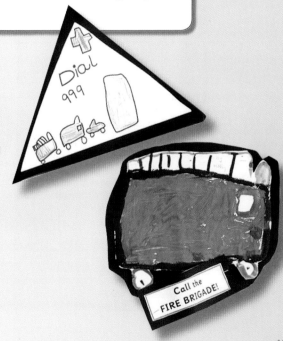

Keeping my feelings safe

Focus of Learning

Recognising and dealing with hurt feelings

Rain clouds make me feel sad and miserable!

Starting Points

- Talk with the children about times when they feel really good, which could be described as 'on top of the world'. Make a list of occasions when the children have felt like this.
- Collect other vocabulary that helps to describe these good feelings, for example, 'great', 'excited', 'happy' and 'brilliant'. (Include current jargon for feeling good.)
- Discuss what it is like when our feelings are hurt. What do people say and do to hurt our feelings?
- Remind the children that when our bodies are hurt we can show people what hurts and be given a plaster or some medicine, but when our feelings are hurt no one can see it.

Sunshine makes me feel HAPPY!

Activities

- Talk about how different feelings might look if we could see them. Ask the children to choose a feeling and illustrate it as we might see it. (For example, a sun for happy, a rain cloud for sad.)
- Identify the things that we can do to help us feel better when our feelings are hurt, such as talking to somebody, listening to music or playing our favourite game.
- What can we do if we have hurt someone else's feelings? Talk about saying sorry and showing we mean it by making sure we don't do it again.
- Make 'feelings boxes' from cuboids. Paint and decorate with beads and collage materials. Line the box with tissue paper. Ask the children to place an object in the box that reminds them of a happy time. Alternatively, children could draw a picture or put some writing in the box.
- Display the boxes surrounded by labels that describe happy feelings. Nearby, add the children's advice about what to do if we hurt someone's feelings.

Keeping our environment safe

Starting Points

- Talk with the class about the local council and its role in keeping the environment safe.
- Present them with this scenario: 'Following many recent complaints, the local council is meeting to decide how to improve the play park so that it is a safer, happier and healthier place for children to play.'
- Ask the children to suggest the kinds of complaints people might have made, for example, vandalism, use by older youths, unsafe swings, dog dirt and litter.

Focus of Learning

 Contributing towards a healthier environment

Activities

- Discuss the ways in which the children could help to keep the park a healthier, safer and happier place to play. Collect their suggestions, such as providing more things for children to do, some places to sit and talk with friends, and more litter bins.
- Invite the class to design signs to display in the park to help combat some of the problems. For example, 'Please keep our park beautiful'.
- Create a display depicting the park. Display the children's signs next to problem areas.

Healthy people

Focus of Learning

Extending children's understanding of health and healthy lifestyles

Starting Points

- Without any discussion, invite the children to draw a picture of a healthy person. Display the pictures in a prominent area ready for debate.

Activities

- Look at the pictures and ask the children to explain how it is possible to tell from their drawings that these are healthy people. What does a healthy person do? How does a healthy person look? How does a healthy person feel? Make a list of their ideas.
- Analyse the ideas and sort them into categories, such as 'Exercise', 'Food', 'Friendship', 'Home and family' and 'Hygiene'.
- Emphasise the importance of health as both physical and emotional well being. Talk about how each category can contribute to a healthy lifestyle.
- Make or paint a large model of a person. Ask the children to show that this person is healthy, for example, by painting on a happy face, dressing in exercise clothes, being outdoors, or with friends.
- Display the model with the children's drawings of healthy people. Add large statements with advice for achieving a healthy lifestyle.

Who helps me be healthy?

Focus of Learning

Understanding that other people are partners in being healthy

Starting Points

- Encourage the children to talk about the people who help them stay healthy. These might include doctors, dentists, the school caretaker, parents, families and school nurses.
- How do they do this? Collect the children's views.
- Take photographs or paint pictures of these people in action.
- Invite some of these people to visit the school and talk about their work.

Activities

- Look at the photographs or pictures and ask the class to imagine what life would be like without these people doing their work. For example, the school would be dirty without a caretaker. Talk about why we need these people to help keep us healthy.
- Explore the ways in which the children can take responsibility for their own health. How can they help the people who are trying to keep them healthy? For example, by remembering to wash their hands.
- Paint large pictures of these people and display them with a sign explaining what each person does to help the children to be healthy.

Food for life

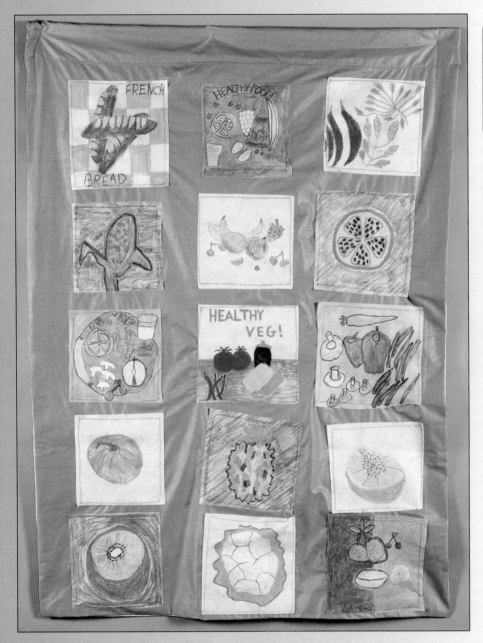

Starting Points

- Talk about when, where and why we eat and drink, and who chooses what we eat. Avoid describing food as 'good' and 'bad', 'healthy' or unhealthy', but instead explain that a healthy diet comprises all kinds of foods – in moderation. Bear in mind cultural differences, children who may be vegetarian, diabetic or who have food intolerances or allergies.

Activities

- Discuss food that helps us to grow and gives us energy and vitality. The children could bring in food packets or pictures to make a display in the classroom.
- Can the class use their scientific knowledge to give examples of food that provide energy, strong bones, healthy insides and skin?
- Emphasise the importance of a balanced diet (not dieting) as a healthy way of eating.
- Ask each child to choose one piece of healthy food to illustrate on a wall hanging. Use batik or draw this image onto a square of fabric.
- Join all the panels together to make a wall hanging. Names of the food could also be sewn onto the hanging.

Fruit is fun

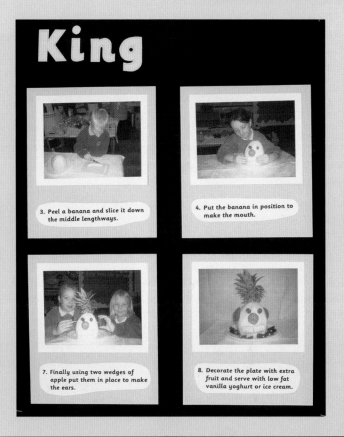

Starting Points

- Bring a selection of fruits into school and talk about the different colours and textures.
- Make a picture collection of different fruits. Prompt the children to find pictures of unusual fruits in magazines and recipe books.

Focus of Learning

 Exploring the role of fruits and vegetables in a healthy diet

Activities

- Talk about the benefits of eating fruits and vegetables for health. Discuss how they help us to stay healthy as they contain vitamins, such as vitamin C, vital for good skin, hair and fighting illness.
- Check that no child is allergic to fruits. Emphasise the importance of food hygiene – that is, wash the fruit, hands and knives before eating. Then taste some of the fruits and make a chart to show preferences.

- Ask the children how else they could sort the fruits, for example, by colour, where they grow, whether they have seeds, etc.
- Make papier-mâché fruits. Use reference books to find out their origins and write about where they come from and how they taste.
- Hang the fruits to make a mobile with the sign 'Eat fruit, keep healthy'. Display the mobile in the dining area.
- Create fun fruit recipes. The children can illustrate recipe cards, giving step-by-step instructions on how to make the dish. Talk about how to make the recipes healthier by using less sugar and more fruit.
- Suggest the children keep a 'fruit diary'. Draw a grid onto a piece of paper with one column for each day of the week. Every time they eat a piece of fruit, the children draw a fruit symbol in the appropriate column.

Healthy heart

Focus of Learning

Understanding that exercise is part of a healthy lifestyle

Starting Points

- Ask the children to demonstrate how they would exercise their legs, arms, shoulders and the rest of their bodies. What else are they exercising inside them? (Muscles and their heart.)
- Talk about how important it is to exercise the heart to keep healthy now and in the future.

Activities

- Discuss the different types of exercise the children can do, both indoors and outdoors. For example, to exercise their hearts in the playground, they can try jogging, sprinting, skipping and hopping to increase heart rate. Show the class how to feel and measure their pulse before and after exercise. Explain that a faster heart rate shows that their heart is being exercised.
- Talk with the children about vigorous exercise and what it means – that is, being out of breath but still able to talk. Explain that they need to do some vigorous exercise every day to keep their bodies, especially their hearts and bones, strong.

- Remind the class why they need to rest and cool down after exercise.
- Talk about how we need to do some sort of exercise every day to keep our bodies, and particularly our hearts, healthy.
- Cut out and make a collage of a large heart. Using black paper, cut out large silhouettes of people showing the active games played by the children.
- Display the silhouettes around the heart collage, together with labels naming the games that help keep the heart healthy.

Exercise your body

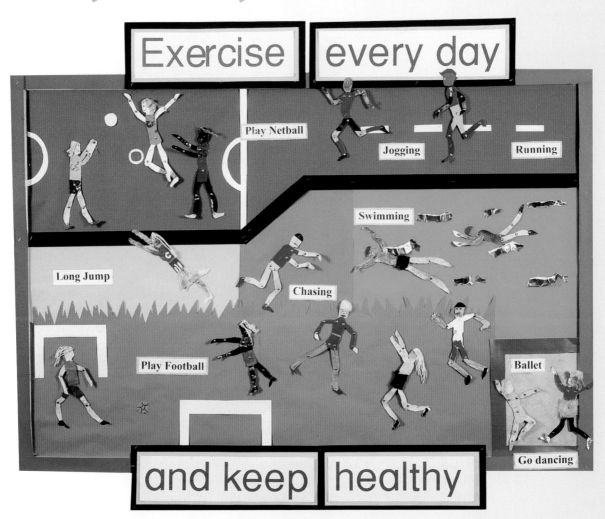

Focus of Learning

Understanding that people vary the kind and amount of exercise they do

Starting Points

- Talk with the children about the different kinds of exercise they do in a day or a week, for example, walking, running, team games and dance.
- Encourage the children to conduct a survey to find out about what types of exercise they do, both in and out of school. Talk about what is involved in carrying out a survey and the questions they need to ask to get this information.

Activities

- Discuss the results from the survey and collate them onto a chart. Which is the most popular form of exercise? The children could use a computer data-handling package to present the findings.
- Demonstrate how to draw a figure with separate limbs. Cut out each limb and join together with split-pins to make movable joints. Make cardboard, split-pin figures with movable joints. Dress the figures using fabric.
- Display the figures to simulate different types of exercises and activities, perhaps adding appropriate accessories.

51

Targets for health

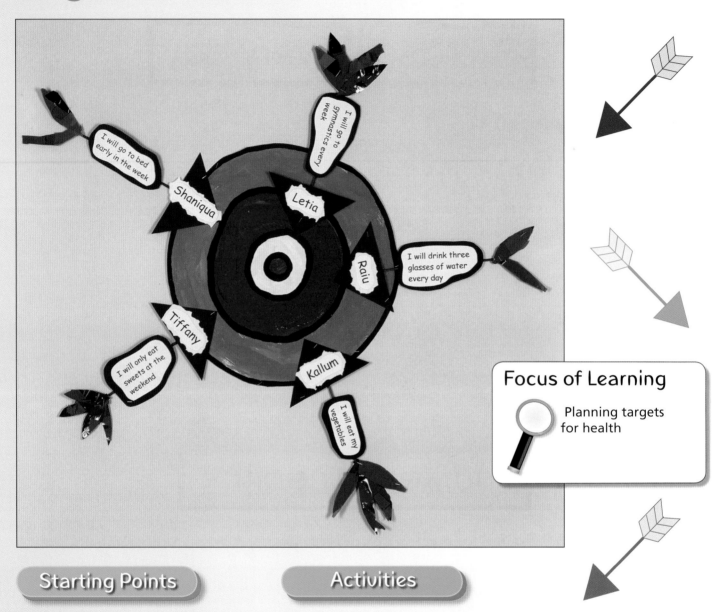

Focus of Learning

Planning targets for health

Starting Points

- Talk about the word 'lifestyle'. Ask children to describe their own lifestyle, focusing particularly on diet, exercise, sleep and well being. Talk about how these four areas contribute to a healthy lifestyle.

- Devise a multiple choice magazine-style quiz to find out whether people in the class think they have a healthy lifestyle. Use questions such as: How often do you exercise?

  a) a lot   b) now and then
  c) not enough

- Invite the children to share their answers and discuss the improvement each of them could make. Call this their target.

Activities

- Discuss the ways in which the children could change their lifestyles to make themselves healthier. For example, eating at least five portions of fruits and vegetables every day, drinking plenty of water, cutting down on sweets and taking exercise.

- Make 'target arrows' from a triangle of card and wooden dowel. Stick the triangle and the dowel together to make an arrow and add feathers. Stick the health target to the arrow.

- Display the arrows pointing towards a target board.

- Link this with a school health week to promote healthy eating, feeling good, exercise and rest as part of a balanced, healthy lifestyle.

Health detectives

Focus of Learning

Understanding the concept of a healthy school Evaluating their school in these terms

Starting Points

- Ask the children to imagine that they are health detectives who are going to investigate how healthy their school is. Make a list of the various areas around school that will need investigation. Under each area, collect the children's ideas on what makes a healthy school. Encourage the class to think about the appearance of the environment, hygiene, safety, and how people's behaviour affects others.

- Follow a detective trail around the school to investigate each area, using the children's ideas. Walk around the school, noting each piece of evidence found.

Is yours a healthy school?

Be a detective. Follow the trail.

1. Go to the playground. Do you see …
   a) happy children playing
   b) no litter
   c) fun games
   d) no bullying?

2. Go to the toilets. Do you see …
   a) clean sinks
   b) people washing their hands
   c) litter in the bin
   d) flushed toilets?

3. Go in a classroom. Do you see …
   a) children working together
   b) children and teachers helping each other
   c) classroom rules
   d) no bullying?

Add up the clues. Is yours a healthy school?

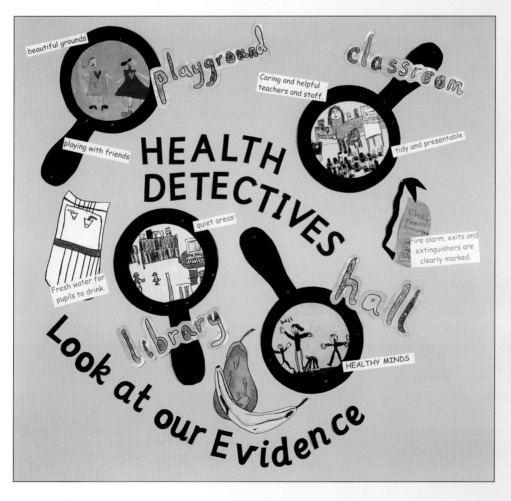

Activities

- Discuss the results of the detective trail. Which are the healthiest places around school? How could the children improve other areas?

- On circular paper, paint large pictures of each area showing the healthy evidence.

- Frame the pictures with magnifying glasses cut out from black paper and acetate.

- Display the magnifying glasses together with labels explaining the evidence found.

- Plan ways in which the class could help to work on areas in the school that need improvement.

Clean and healthy

- Talk with the children about how it feels to be hot, sweaty, dirty and dusty after being outdoors for a day. What do they do when they feel like that? Collect and list their ideas. How do they feel when they are clean?

Focus of Learning

Heightening awareness of personal hygiene

Activities

- How do the children keep themselves clean and healthy? For example, baths, showers, wearing clean clothes, brushing their hair, cutting their nails and cleaning their teeth. Illustrate some of these 'keeping clean' routines.

- Talk about germs and how they are invisible and can be passed on to other people. Discuss how germs and viruses can make us ill. Make a list of ways to help prevent the spread of germs and illness, such as using a tissue when sneezing and washing hands after going to the toilet. Paint large pictures to illustrate each idea.

- Design posters to illustrate ways of avoiding the spread of germs. It is important to make these positive, not all 'don'ts' by using 'Remember to … ', 'Try to … ', 'Make sure to … ' instead.

Persuasion

Focus of Learning

Dealing with positive and negative persuasion

Starting Points

- Tell the children the story of Max.

- Talk with the children about who they think tried to persuade Max on each day of the week, what the person might have said and how they tried to persuade him.

Activities

- Discuss the two kinds of persuasion: to persuade someone to do something good and to persuade someone to do something that could be wrong or dangerous.

- Talk about the kinds of persuasion that people sometimes use to encourage others to do something wrong or dangerous. Discuss the possible outcomes of listening to these kinds of persuasion.

On **Monday** someone tried to persuade Max to clean his teeth.

On **Tuesday** someone tried to persuade Max to eat his dinner.

On **Wednesday** someone tried to persuade Max to finish writing his story.

On **Thursday** someone tried to persuade Max to cross the road in the wrong place.

On **Friday** someone tried to persuade Max to take a biscuit from the tin.

On **Saturday** someone tried to persuade Max to go off and play without telling Mum.

On **Sunday** someone tried to persuade Max to try his inline skates.

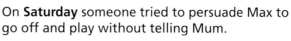

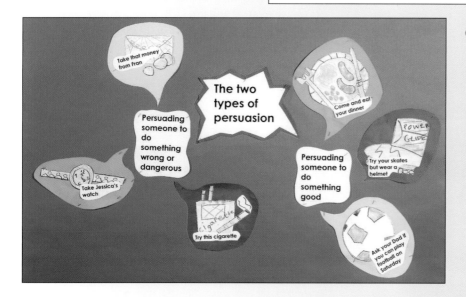

- Ask the children to illustrate the two different kinds of persuasion – that is, persuading someone to do something good and something that could be dangerous or wrong.

What goes into our bodies?

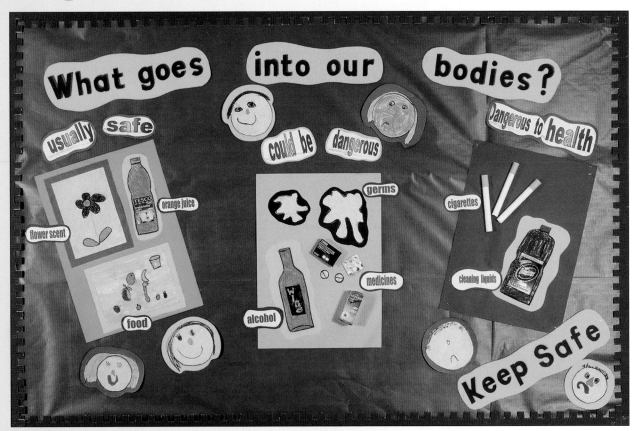

Starting Points

- Ask the children to talk about and list all the things that go into their bodies, and how those things get in (for example, splinters, germs, food, smoke, tablets, smells, dust, ointment and injections).
- With the whole class, sort their ideas into categories, such as those things that get in through the nose, ears, eyes, mouth or skin.

Focus of Learning

Increasing awareness of what goes into their bodies and some of the possible dangers

Activities

- Talk with the children about things:
  - that are unavoidable
  - that they have some control over
  - that someone might try to persuade them to take or use.
- Encourage the class to categorise the items again, but this time under the headings: 'Usually safe', 'Could be dangerous' and 'Dangerous to our health'.

- Divide a board into three columns. Ask the children to draw pictures of the items discussed above and place them with a label in the correct column. This would be a good opportunity to remind the children of the correct procedures if they find any pills, medicines, needles or syringes, and to reinforce the dangers of picking these up.

Being ill – getting better

Starting Points

- Discuss whether anyone in the class, including yourself, has had to take medicines recently. Talk about what was wrong, the kinds of medicines they took, how the medicines made them feel and where the medicines came from.

Activities

- Acknowledge the fact that all medicines contain drugs which change what is happening inside your body. Talk about the dangers of medicines and remind the children of the following safety rules:
  - Only take the right amount
  - Only take medicine from a trusted adult
  - Do not take anyone else's medicine
  - Read the labels carefully and follow the instructions
  - Keep medicines safely out of the reach of young children.

Focus of Learning

Recognising the role of medicines and understanding that all medicines are drugs

- Examine some empty medicine packets and point out where to find the instructions. Make a medicine cabinet from junk materials and construct medicine packets from cuboids.

- Display the packets inside the cabinet. Ask the children to make signs about keeping medicines safe and hang these around the cabinet. Rather than producing a series of 'don'ts', encourage the class to use the words: 'Remember … ' 'Think … ', 'Ask … ', 'Remind … ', 'Warn … ' and 'Keep safe … '.

- You could invite the school nurse or other health professional in to talk about childhood ailments. Who and what helps to make the patient feel better?

I can say 'no'

Focus of Learning

Understanding that substances can be misused with consequences for health and behaviour

Starting Points

- Ask the children to work with a partner – one to draw a picture of someone trying to persuade a child to smoke a cigarette, the other to draw a similar picture but replacing the cigarettes with alcohol. Share their pictures in a class discussion about the persuasive language that may be used in each situation.
- Collect the children's suggestions, writing them in speech bubbles.

Activities

- Talk with the children about the ways in which they could refuse to join in something they don't wish to do. Would it be easy? Collect and record their views. Use this opportunity for the children to practise their suggestions of how they would refuse to be persuaded.
- Ask the children, 'What other substances might people try to persuade you to sniff, take or taste?' Where appropriate, this could be an opportunity to distinguish between legal substances that contain

helpful drugs (such as medicines) and legal drugs (such as nicotine and alcohol), and illegal substances.

- Make a collage of a figure of a child and create masks to represent other people. On one side of the figure, add some masks and the children's speech bubbles illustrating the persuasive language from the earlier discussion. On the other side, add masks with positive statements showing what the central figure could say and do to deal positively with this persuasion.

Smoking

Starting Points

- Ask the children to imagine themselves in a room where a lot of people are smoking cigarettes. Encourage them to think of two or three words to describe how the smoke makes them feel. Where in their bodies is the smoke going?

- Prompt everyone to share their views first with a partner and then in groups. Then, as a class, collect a list of their words and phrases.

Activities

- Talk with the children about people for whom smoking cigarettes can be particularly dangerous (for example, pregnant women, babies, people with breathing problems and people training for sports). Explain that this is because cigarettes contain a drug called nicotine.

- Suggest the children draw someone who is thinking of starting to smoke and write why the person is thinking of doing this. Remind them to add reasons for not smoking.

- Make a display with examples of current health warnings found on cigarette packets. Make a model cigarette packet and surround this with the children's views on smoking. Add leaflets about giving up smoking.

- Talk with the children about available sources of reliable health information, for example, the school nurse and doctor's surgery. Put copies of this information on the display. Invite these people into school to support the work.

Facts or opinions?

Starting Points

- Introduce two characters, Sam and Jo. They see some of their friends smoking cigarettes and ask them why they do it. Some of the answers are: 'Everyone does it', 'You look cool', 'It makes you look grown up', 'It's easy to stop when you want to'.

- Ask the class to suggest some more reasons for smoking that friends might give. These could be written in speech bubbles and attached to the wall as the discussion progresses.

Activities

- Tackle each of these statements with the children – working as a class or in pairs – to decide whether the reasons given are facts or people's opinions. Remind the children that what they see and read in the media is not always true, even when it is convincingly presented.

- Create a photo story with your own characters showing how to resist persuasion to try a cigarette. Use a digital camera to generate the photo images.

- Role-play the scenarios with the class.

JADE'S CASEBOOK DIARY

Jade set off for school.

Hi Jade.

Oh hi Anna.

Fancy a fag?

No thanks, it's bad for you.

It's fun.

Yeah, go on it's cool.

Go on everyone does it.

And aren't we little Miss Perfect?

Look I've said it once, NO!

Oh yes lardy da!

What was that all about?

They were trying to make me smoke!

Hi Hannah!

Yuck! They're so immature.

Pressure, pressure, pressure

Starting Points

- Prompt the children to think about the different kinds of advertising posters they see around them where they live – such as those advertising events, places to visit, things to eat or things to buy. Do any of them begin with 'Don't' or 'Say "No" to …'?
- What are these posters trying to persuade people to do? Collect the children's ideas, for example, 'come', 'buy', 'try' and 'visit'.

Focus of Learning

Extending understanding of persuasion and pressure, and the strategies for dealing with this

Activities

- Remind the class that people both in and out of school try to persuade them to keep themselves healthy by, for example, cleaning their teeth, crossing roads carefully, eating more fruit and vegetables, running and walking about more, and not falling out with their friends. Does everyone try to do these things?
- Now explain that people can try to persuade others to do things that are dangerous, such as going off without telling anyone, riding a bicycle without a helmet, sniffing or tasting something dangerous or illegal. Sometimes these people keep on and on, trying to persuade you so that it feels as if you are being pushed into doing it. This is called pressure.

- Ask the children to think of ways of standing up to this pressure, for example, by walking away, telling someone or saying 'I don't do that'. Collect the examples and display these to help others.
- Draw or paint large posters to encourage others to resist pressure.

Rules around school

Focus of Learning

Understanding the need for rules in school and the wider community

Starting Points

- Take the class for a walk in and around your school, looking for all the notices that are rules.

- Talk with the children about the rules found. Examples might include: 'No parking', 'Visitors, please report to reception', 'Silence: this is a quiet area', 'No smoking', 'Put litter in the bin', 'Please walk, don't run', 'Please put your books here'.

- Discuss who made the rules. Who are they for – parents, children, teachers or visitors to the school? Why do we have these rules in school?

Activities

- Illustrate some rules and the places where the children found them.

- Chat about how rules help to keep all the people in the school safe, healthy, happy and friendly, and how, if everyone keeps to the rules, it is fair to everyone.

- Point out that good citizens understand why rules are needed and try to keep them. Remind the class that they each have a responsibility to do the same.

- Encourage everyone to think of other places they visit, such as libraries, shopping centres, swimming pools or football stadia. Can they think of the rules in these places and say why they have them?

Breaking the rules

I hit somebody

I swear in school

I steal somebody else's property

I bully somebody

I am rude to a teacher

I deliberately don't follow instructions

Starting Points

- Ask the children why they sometimes break the rules. How do they feel when they know they are breaking a rule?

Activities

- Cut out pictures of people from magazines and add speech bubbles to illustrate the feelings associated with breaking the rules.
- Talk about the sanctions or penalties in place in your school. Why are they needed? Make a lift-the-flap chart to illustrate the sanctions and rules that go with them for your class.
- Brainstorm some rules made by the local council or the country's legal system. What happens if people break these rules? Consider the implications of breaking the rules in school, in the local area and nationally.

Focus of Learning

 Understanding the need for sanctions in school and the wider community

Pocket Park campaign

- Look at photographs of some local areas near to your school. Who keeps these areas looking good? What evidence is there to show that they are well looked after?
- How does an area become spoilt? List the children's suggestions.
- Talk about any areas near to the school where the children may have seen these problems.
- Read the story of the 'Pocket Park Campaign', as reported in the *Park News* newspaper. Talk about how this kind of vandalism hurts both wildlife and everyone who enjoys the place.

Activities

- Ask the children what they would do about Pocket Park. Turn this into an action plan for cleaning up the park.
- Create posters for Pocket Park to help make people aware of the problems.
- Talk about how this could be linked with local and national campaigns.

Focus of Learning

Exploring ways of tackling local environmental problems

PARK NEWS

Today we heard the shocking story of Pocket Park, the famous beauty spot close to Park Primary School.

The children at this school have been caring for this lovely place, looking after the wild flowers and pond life.

Yesterday the children went down to the park with their teachers to see if the ducklings had hatched. To their horror they saw litter everywhere, even in the water! There were signs that people had been fishing and swimming.

The *Park News* and the children have started a campaign to stop this vandalism. Will you help? If you can, please speak to the school.

Changing places

Starting Points

- Ask the children to think about their classroom at the end of a day when they have been doing a lot of creative activities, such as painting, modelling clay or making displays. Can they picture the scene in their heads?

- Now ask them to imagine their classroom with everything clean, tidy and cared for, with all the rubbish collected. How would they feel if someone came into their classroom, tipped out the rubbish and broke things they had made to spoil their display?

Focus of Learning

Understanding that people's behaviour impacts on the environment

Activities

- Prompt the children to talk about some of their favourite places to play. What do good citizens do to help to keep these places safe and healthy?

- What do people do to spoil these places? Discuss whether this is deliberate vandalism or whether it's just that no one has bothered to take care of the place. Collect the children's ideas and discuss why it is difficult to stop these things happening and what people could do.

- Encourage the class to collect pictures from local newspapers, to take photographs or to paint pictures of places where people are spoiling the environment. Make these into a 'Before' display.

- Discuss what good citizens could do to change these places into healthier, happier environments. Help them to make this into an 'After' display.

Citizens of the world

Citizen

A citizen of a place is someone who was born there or lives there **citizenship**(noun) the rights of a citizen.

Starting Points

- Talk about how the world is represented as a map or as a globe. Can the children find their own country, city or town on a globe or map?

Focus of Learning

Exploring the concept of world citizenship

Activities

- Explain that just as we are citizens of our own country, so we are citizens of the world because our country is part of this world as they have seen on the map.

- Create a 'citizens of the world' map using cut-out pictures of faces stuck onto an outline of a world map. They could include a picture of themselves.

- Ask the children to look through their class and school libraries and make a display of maps, globes and books showing people from all around the world. Mix information books, poetry and stories.

- Explain to the class that we are all citizens of the world with rights and responsibilities. We need to respect and care about other people's cultures, religions and lifestyles.

Learning to be good citizens

Focus of Learning

Identifying the challenges of becoming good citizens

Starting Points

- Talk with the children about all the people in their school who help to make the school a good place for everyone. What do they all do? Collect their ideas.

Activities

- Talk about the different jobs these people have and what the children can do to make these jobs easier and better for everyone.

- Discuss people outside school, such as family, friends, school staff, people at church, police officers and others who help to keep them safe, healthy and happy. Remind the children that working together, whether in or out of school, is what good citizens do.

- Ask the children what they are doing to show that they are good citizens. What do they need to get better at? Make a list and ask the children to vote on which they think are the most important challenges.

- Write these challenges onto decorated card discs and hang them together to make a mobile for the whole class.

- Encourage the children to review the challenges each week and discuss how close they are to success. They could hang stars under any challenges achieved.

- Explain that everyone's contribution in society makes for a better, happier, healthier and safer place to be. Their efforts make villages, towns and cities better places to live, and this is all part of being good citizens.

Children's literature as a resource

Our work with children has shown that what they see as sensitive issues affecting their physical and emotional well being are not always those perceived as such by adults. Many adults regard issues of sex and relationships, misuse of substances, child abuse, bullying, culture and gender issues, bereavement and loss as the main areas where care is necessary. This is not to say these issues are not painful for children – especially those who are affected by them – but to note that children have other sensitivities, too.

Children's sensitivities stem from their need to be valued, to be secure, to be listened to and to be heard. When we asked children what they wanted to be able to talk about with adults, freely and safely, they said they wanted to talk about their feelings and other people's, about growing up, change, parting, separation, loss, grief, death, leaving childhood behind, love – being in love and out of love – and much more.

The children struggled for words to help them express fears, frustrations, delight, jealousy, hope, remorse, uncertainty, joy, conflict and empathy. We saw their feelings in their faces and bodies, yet for many the language they had was confined to feeling 'mad', 'bad', 'sad' or 'glad'. Children need help to acquire and develop a language of feelings so they can talk confidently about, and understand the impact of, feelings on their own and other people's actions.

Children's literature can provide us with a unique setting for developing a language of feelings, especially when we read to them. In a story we can share a whole range of human emotions through the feelings of each character – we can get inside their problems and be critical of their decisions. We can discover what the characters have learned about themselves, and about other people. We can even learn about ourselves when we see ourselves reflected in the story. By using a book we can take the children into a world beyond their day-to-day lives, to places and situations we would never dream of taking them in real life. We can sense and feel danger ahead, and share the sense of risk and fear. We can be ahead of the characters, see danger before they do and see the critical moment when they make a decision that affects the story's ending. We can experience all this as if it was really happening, safe in the knowledge that it is only a story and soon the book will be closed. No one will criticise us for what we thought, felt or said.

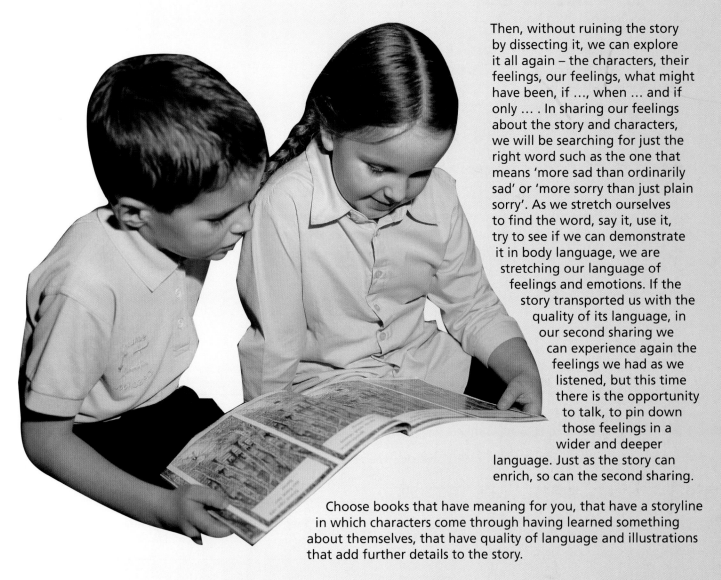

Then, without ruining the story by dissecting it, we can explore it all again – the characters, their feelings, our feelings, what might have been, if …, when … and if only … . In sharing our feelings about the story and characters, we will be searching for just the right word such as the one that means 'more sad than ordinarily sad' or 'more sorry than just plain sorry'. As we stretch ourselves to find the word, say it, use it, try to see if we can demonstrate it in body language, we are stretching our language of feelings and emotions. If the story transported us with the quality of its language, in our second sharing we can experience again the feelings we had as we listened, but this time there is the opportunity to talk, to pin down those feelings in a wider and deeper language. Just as the story can enrich, so can the second sharing.

Choose books that have meaning for you, that have a storyline in which characters come through having learned something about themselves, that have quality of language and illustrations that add further details to the story.

Look with great care at books written all too obviously to put across someone's view of a sensitive issue or books which inform – it takes a brilliant author to inform successfully. Use information books as a resource in book corners and libraries, and find a place for 'issue' books there. Their purpose is different and children will want to pick from these resources as necessary.

Children's literature is a very different resource. Each story will lend itself to questions such as:

– What would you have felt if you had seen this happening?
– What would you have wanted to say to them?
– What would you have wanted to do?
– What if you had been one of them? Would you have felt differently?
– What if it had been two boys instead of two girls?
– What if the problem had been … ? What might have happened?

Thus, with questions and possibilities, you can turn the storyline to any problem. You and the children can peel away layer upon layer without ever spoiling the story and its magic. Remember, though, to put the story together again at the end. Reread it or choose the 'best bit' to read once more. Leave a few quiet moments at the end before you move on.

Give the class the best in children's literature and they will come back for more. As you share the story first time round, then again, they and you will share a brief magic moment, and they may find a new and better 'language of feelings'.

Recommended literature

Title	Author(s)	Publisher	Date
A New Home for Tiger	Joan Stimson	Scholastic Children's Books	1998
A Piece of Cake	Jill Murphy	Walker Books	1998
Amazing Grace	Mary Hoffman	Frances Lincoln	1993
Badger on the Barge	Janni Howker	Walker Books	1989
Badger's Parting Gifts	Susan Varley	Collins Picture Lions	1992
Being Friends	Althea	A & C Black	2001
Being Kind	Janine Amos & Annabel Spenceley (Illustrator)	Cherry Tree Books	2001
Bill's New Frock	Anne Fine	Egmont Books	1990
Can't You Sleep Little Bear?	Martin Waddell	Walker Books	2000
Changes	Anthony Browne	Walker Books	1995
Comfort Herself	Geraldine Kaye	Scholastic Point Books	1997
Dear Daddy	Philippe Dupasquier	Anderson Press	2002
Dr Xargles Book of Earthlets	Jeanne Willis	Red Fox	1990
Emma's Lamb	Kim Lewis	Walker Books	1992
Five Minutes' Peace	Jill Murphy	Walker Books	1986
Flour Babies	Anne Fine	Puffin Books	1994
Goodnight Mister Tom	Michelle Magorian	Harper Collins Children's	1982
Grandma's Bill	Martin Waddell	Hodder Wayland	1991
Growing Pains	Jenny Stow	Frances Lincoln	1996
Hue Boy	Rita Phillips Mitchell	Puffin Books	1997
I Hate Roland Roberts	Martina Selway	Red Fox	1995
I'll Always Love You	Hans Wilhelm	Hodder Children's Books	1985
I'll Take You to Mrs Cole	Nigel Gray	Andersen Press	1988
I'm Sorry	Sam McBratney	Collins Picture Lions	2001
John Brown, Rose and the Midnight Cat	Jenny Wagner	Viking Children's Books	1977
Just Like Us	Hiawyn Oram	Corgi	1990
Leaving Mrs Ellis	Catherine Robinson	Red Fox	1997
Making Friends	Margaret Mahy	Penguin	1991
Not Now Bernard	David McKee	Red Fox	1996
Nothing	Mick Inkpen	Hodder Children's Books	1996
Once There Were Giants	Martin Waddell	Walker Books	2001
Orlando's Little-While Friends	Audrey Wood	Child's Play International	1989
Red Sky in the Morning	Elizabeth Laird	Macmillan Children's	1989
Ruby	Maggie Glen	Red Fox	1992
Six Dinner Sid	Inga Moore	Hodder Children's Books	2000
Something Else	Kathryn Cave	Puffin Books	1995
Stranger Danger?	Anne Fine	Puffin Books	2000
Taking Turns	Janine Amos & Annabel Spenceley (Illustrator)	Cherry Tree Books	2001
Terrible Tuesday	Hazel Townson	Andersen Press	1999
The Angel of Nitshill Road	Anne Fine	Mammoth Books	1993
The Bad-Tempered Ladybird	Eric Carle	Puffin Books	2000
The Bed and Breakfast Star	Jacqueline Wilson	Yearling	1995
The Dark at the Top of the Stairs	Sam McBratney	Walker Books	1997
The Egg Man (from Badger on the Barge)	Janni Howker	Walker Books	1996
The Gorilla Who Wanted to Grow Up	Jill Tomlinson	Mammoth Books	1991
The Huge Bag of Worries	Virginia Ironside	McDonald Young Books	1996
The Owl Who Was Afraid of the Dark	Jill Tomlinson	Mammoth Books	1991
The Suitcase Kid	Jacqueline Wilson	Yearling	1993
The True Story of the Three Little Pigs	Jon Scieszka	Puffin Books	1991
The Very Hungry Caterpillar	Eric Carle	Puffin Books	1974
The Very Worst Monster	Pat Hutchins	Red Fox	1996
The Year of the Worm	Ann Pilling	Lion Publishing	2000
This is Our House	Michael Rosen	Walker Books	1998
Two Monsters	David McKee	Red Fox	1997
We are Best Friends	Aliki	Econoclad Books	1999
We're Going on a Bear Hunt	Michael Rosen	Walker Books	1993
What Can I Write?	Martina Selway	Red Fox	1998
Where's My Teddy?	Jez Alborough	Walker Books	1994
Who are your Friends?	Jillian Powell	Hodder Wayland	1996
Why is the Sky Blue?	Sally Grindley	Andersen Press	1996
Wilfred Gordon McDonald Partridge	Mem Fox	Puffin Books	1987
Willy the Wimp	Anthony Browne	Walker Books	1995

Please note that this list gives UK publishers. Readers in other territories will need to check the local publisher.

For details of further Belair publications, please write to
BELAIR PUBLICATIONS LIMITED,
Apex Business Centre,
Boscombe Road, Dunstable, LU5 4 RL
or email folens@folens.com

For sales and distribution in North America and South America,
INCENTIVE PUBLICATIONS,
3835 Cleghorn Avenue, Nashville, Tn 37215,
USA.

For sales and distribution in Australia,
EDUCATIONAL SUPPLIES PTY LTD,
8 Cross Street, Brookvale, NSW 2100,
Australia.

For sales and distribution (in other territories),
FOLENS PUBLISHERS,
Apex Business Centre,
Boscombe Road, Dunstable, LU5 4RL,
United Kingdom.
Email: folens@folens.com
www.folens.com